photo doodles

Photo credits

All images courtesy Fotolia unless otherwise noted.

3 © Karl Barrett/iStock | 4-5 © Lance Bellers | 6-7 © Ljupco Smokovski | 8-9 © stanislav rishnyak/iStock, © Maksym Bondarchuk/iStock | 10-11 © Dominique LUZY | 12-13 © Ingus Evertovskis | 14-15 © Eduardo Rivero | 16-17 © Sergej Khackimullin | 18-19 © RoJo Images | 20-21 © Mrkvica | 22-23 © Eric Isselée, © biglama | 24-25 © dred2010, © Gregor Buir (composited by ViiiZ) | 26-27 © robynmac | 28-29 © kmirgaya | 30-31 © A-G-N-I, © Anyka | 32-33 © Big City Lights | 34-35 © Artsem Martysiuk, © goce risteski, © jazavac, © brozova | 36-37 © Kitch Bain | 38-39 © Art Photo Picture, © Steve Maehl/iStock | 40-41 © Yuri Arcurs | 42-43 © Eric Isselée | 44-45 © Vladimir Voronin, © Dmytro Sukharevskyy, © cantor pannatto, © maryo990, © Sergey, © Jiri Hera | 46-47 © 2d3dmolier, © Ruth Black, © Elenathewise | 48-49 © Cobalt, © Faber Visum | 50-51 © Sergey Ilin, © valdis torms | 52-53 © innovari | 54-55 © Mykola Velychko | 56-57 © Ljupco Smokovski, © Mark Lipson/iStock | 58-59 © Vidady | 60-61 © sellingpix | 62-63 © anankkml, © Smileus | 64-65 © Africa Studio | 66-67 © klikk, © Ljupco Smokovski | 68-69 © Maksim Toome, © Anatoliy Meshkov, © Sergey Lavrentev | 70-71 © DR | 72-73 © verte, © Dmitry Naumov | 74-75 © DR | 76-77 © fotomatrix | 78-79 © Ilya Chalyuk | 80-81 © olly, ©DeoSum |82-83 © filograph | 84-85 © AlexandreNunes, © Burwell and Burwell Photography/iStock | 86-87 © ketsur, © Kirill Kurashov | 88-89 © He2, © Millisenta, © piai | 90-91 © Michael Rosskothen, © Andy Lidstone/iStock | 92-93 © Lisa Thornberg/iStock, © Bruce Lonngren/iStock, © DNY59/iStock | 94-95 © DNY59/iStock, © kyoshino/iStock, © Doris Karlovits/iStock, © Don Nichols/iStock | 96-97 © Amanda Rohde/iStock, © Robert Biedermann/iStock, © Christian Musat/iStock | 98-99 © Marcus Lindström/iStock | 100-101 © magdasmith/iStock, © Grigory Bibikov/iStock, © Ivan Vasilev/iStock | 102-103 © David Hernandez/iStock | 104-105 © Baris Simsek/iStock, © Sarah Salmela/iStock, © Julián Rovagnati/iStock, © maria paz morales/iStock | 106-107 © Bart Coenders/iStock | 108-109 © aguirre_mar/iStock, © ILYA AKINSHIN/iStock | 110-111 © t_kimura/iStock | 112-113 © Richard Partridge/iStock, © Sharon Day/iStock | 114-115 © Catherine Yeulet/iStock, © Trout55/iStock, © Mark Swallow/iStock | 116-117 © Dariusz Kuzminski/iStock, © Marko Skrbic/iStock | 118-119 © Marek Mnich/iStock, © james steidl/iStock | 120-121 © DSGpro/iStock | 122-123 © subjug/iStock, © Dušan Zidar/iStock | 124-125 © Dariusz Kuzminski/iStock, © malerapaso/iStock | 126-127 © Lew Robertson/iStock, © Bill Noll/iStock | 128-129 © Aleksander Trankov/iStock, © David Anderson/iStock, © allanswart/iStock, © Dirk Rietschel/iStock, © Gjermund Alsos/iStock | 130-131 © Björn Magnusson/iStock, © Karl Barrett/iStock | 132-133 © Eric Isselée/iStock | 134-135 © RonTech2000/iStock | 136-137 © Jason Lugo/iStock, © Donna Coleman/iStock | 138-139 © Nigel Carse/iStock | 140-141 © Talaj/iStock | 142-143 © 4x6/iStock, © JOHN GOMEZ/iStock, © yasinguneysu/iStock, © Özgür Donmaz/iStock | 144-145 © Martti Salmela/iStock, © Philip Dyer/iStock | 146-147 © Vernon Wiley/iStock | 148-149 © t_kimura/iStock, © Dimitris Stephanides/iStock, © subjug/iStock | 150-151 © wajan | 152-153 © Neiromobile | 154-155 © FreshPaint | 156-157 © Joan Vicent Cantó Roig/iStock | 158-159 © robybret | 160 © Karl Barrett/iStock

Adapted from the book *Fill in the Blank* by ViiiZ, first published in the United States in 2012.

Library of Congress Cataloging in Publication Number: 2013930161

ISBN: 978-1-59474-652-9

Printed in China

Typeset in Swiss and Liebe Erika

Designed by Katie Hatz, based on a design by ViiiZ
Production management by John J. McGurk

Quirk Books
215 Church Street
Philadelphia, PA 19106
quirkbooks.com

10 9 8 7 6 5 4 3 2 1

photo
doodles

by
ViiiZ

Élodie Chaillous
& Vahram Muratyan

200 pictures
for you to
complete

QUIRK BOOKS

PHILADELPHIA

The kingdom needs a new castle—yours!

Draw the kitten some friends.

Let's put
on a show!

What's up in the sky?

What's in these cans? They need labels!

Who's hungry?

Make a masterpiece.

Bake up some buddies.

These horses need riders …
and a pasture to run in!

Color the kitties' coats.

Who's looking in the mirrors?

Shhh ... write some secret messages.

I LOVE YOU

MEET ME at 5 P.M. – STADIUM

ON AL

Do these heads need hats? Or helmets? Or hairnets?

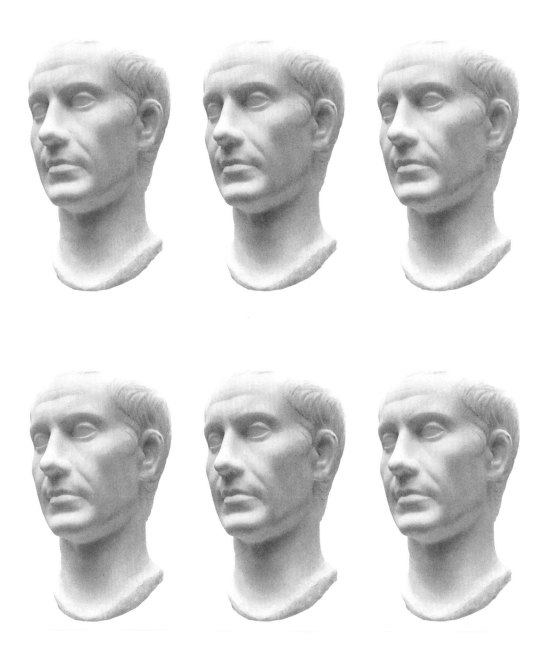

Draw some egg-celent egg decorations.

Rock on! Put your favorite band in the spotlight.

Invent an awesome ride with these wheels.

What's growing in these pots?

Build the best thrill ride ever.

Draw the perfect island paradise.

Make us moo-tiful!

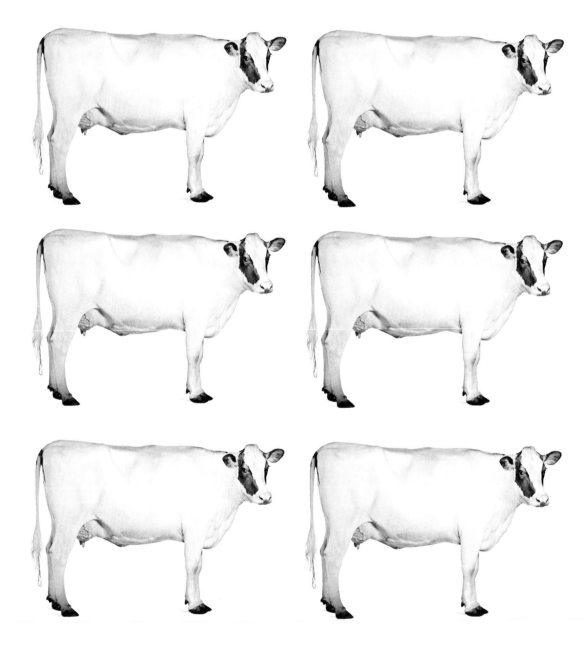

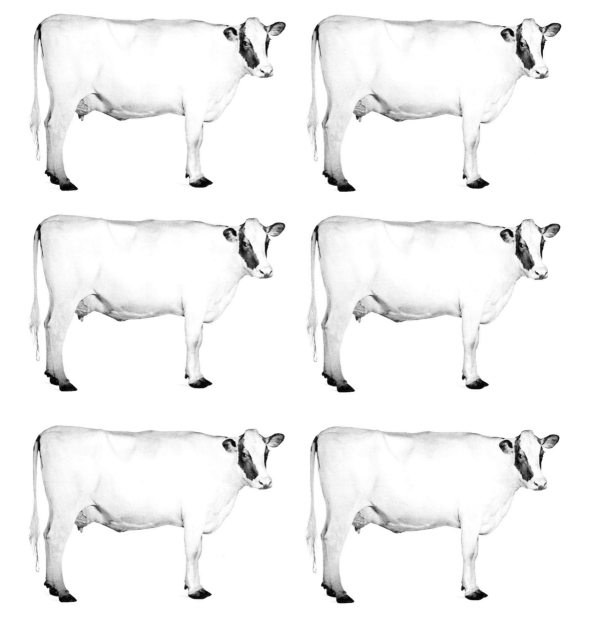

What's for lunch?

Oh, no . . . the bakery forgot to finish these cakes.
Decorate them.

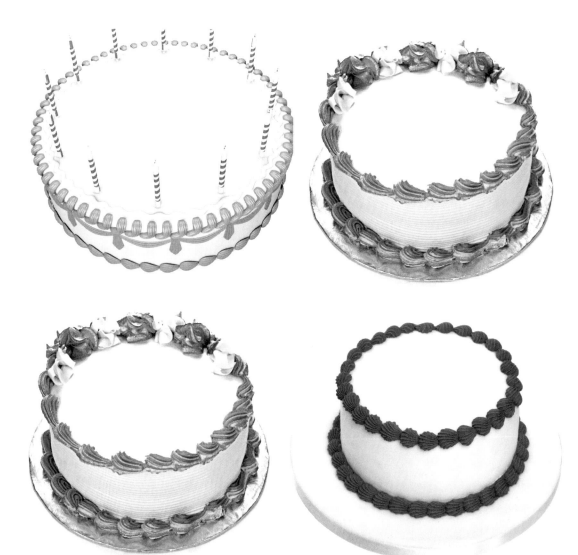

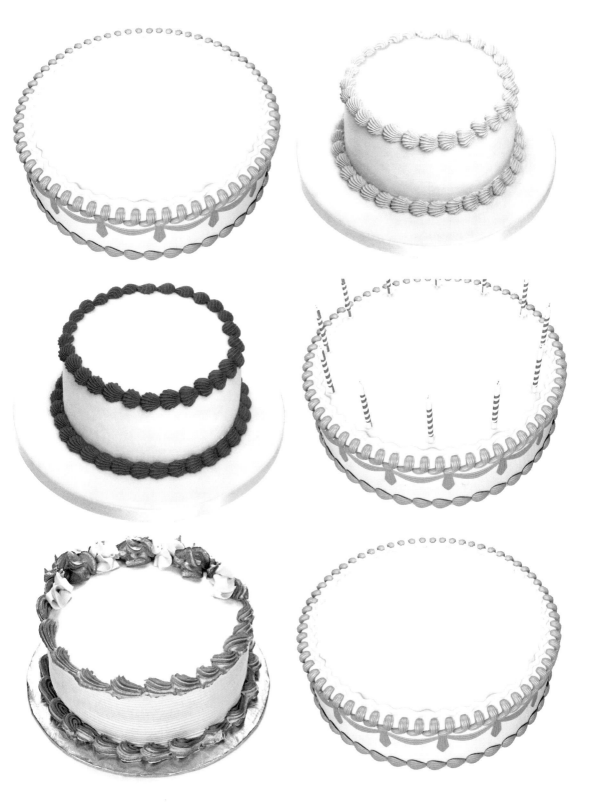

What's on TV? You decide!

Surprise! What popped out of these boxes?

Boldly draw what no one has drawn before.

Give the goldfish some friends to visit.

Reel 'em in! What did they catch?

Make these sneakers snazzy.

What's waiting over the hill?

Fix these animals before the zookeeper shows up!

Scoop up something sweet.

Abracadabra! Something has appeared in the magician's hat. But what?

Customize these cars.

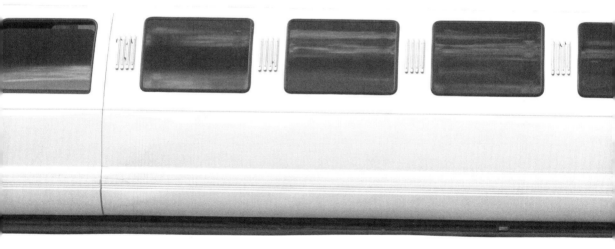

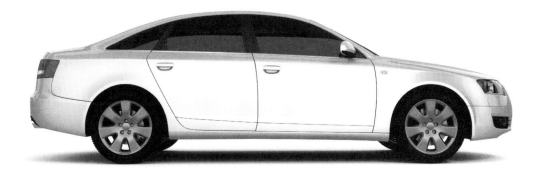

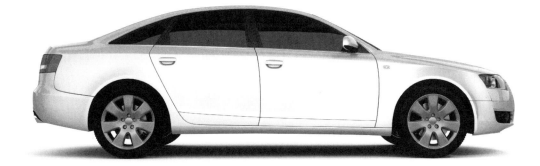

What will you play?

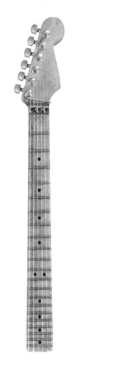

Snack attack! Draw the tastiest treats ever.

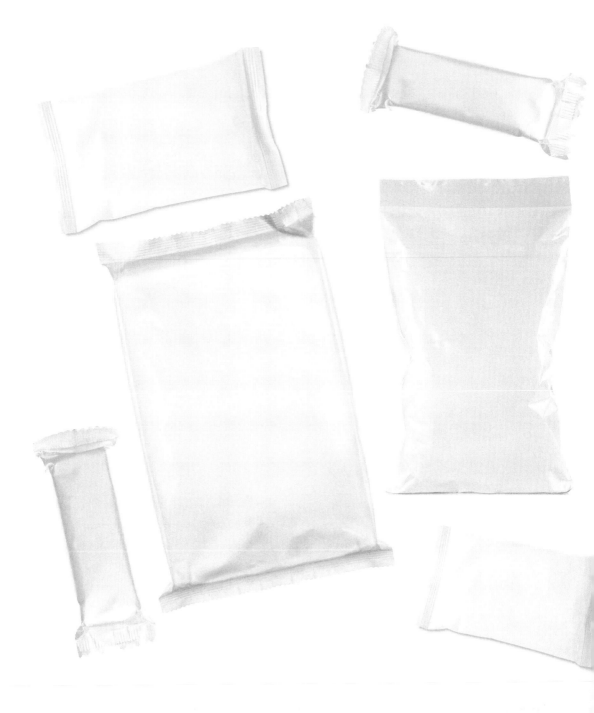

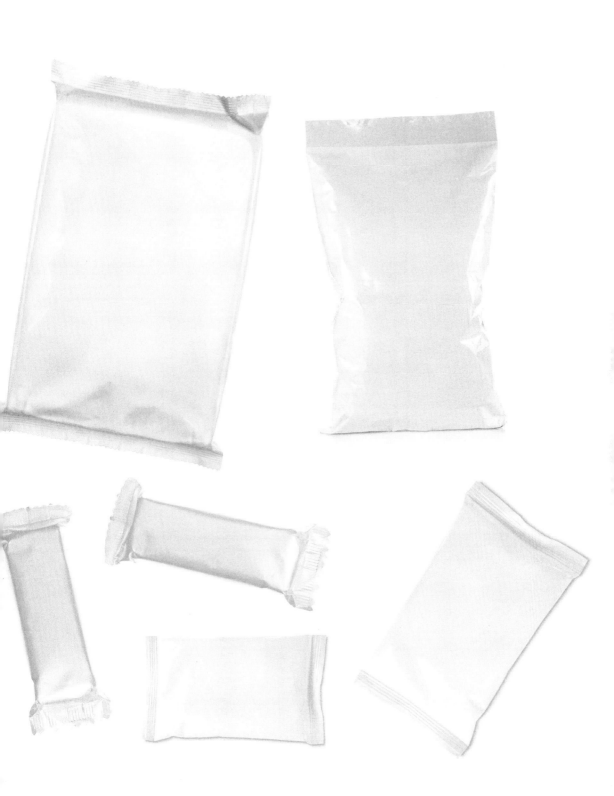

What's the story here? Add words and pictures

to make your own comic strip.

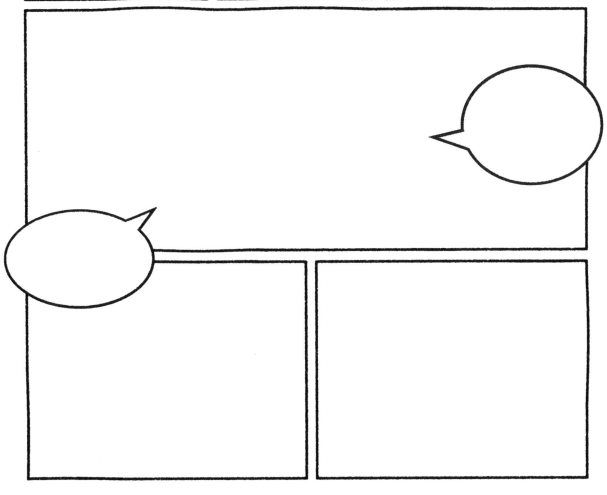

Dress up the dancing dolls.

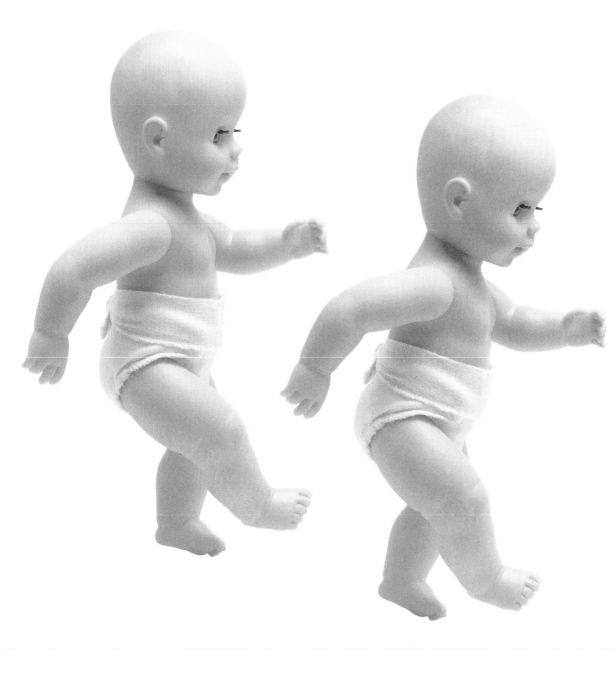

These heads need hair-dos!

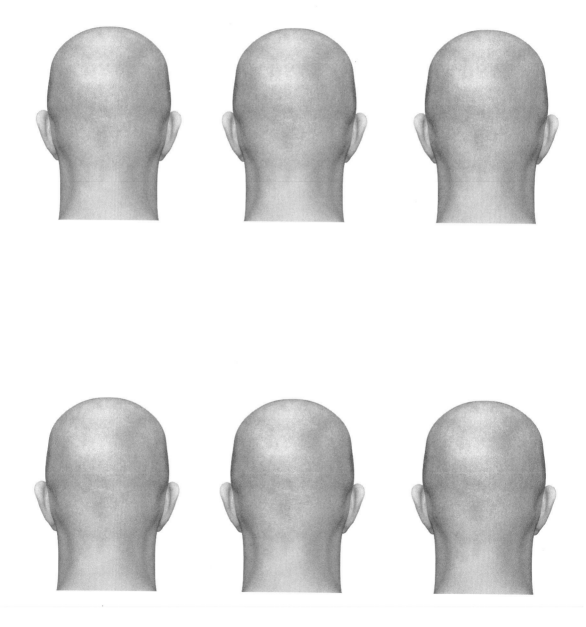

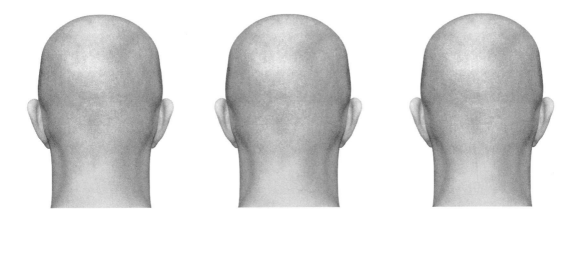

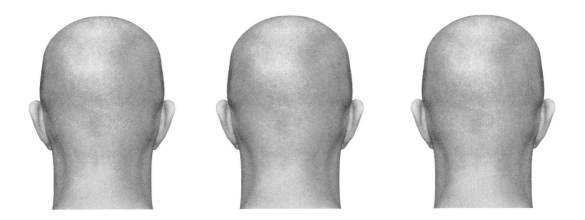

Aliens are here! What do they look like, and who is there to greet them?

Trouble at the umbrella factory! These umbrellas need decorating.

It's your turn at the blackboard . . .
What will you write?

Decorate the nesting dolls before they're tucked away.

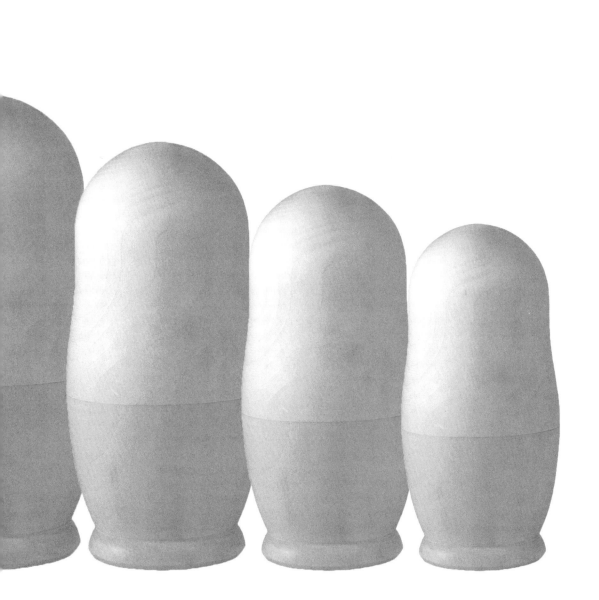

Create a collection of cool caps.

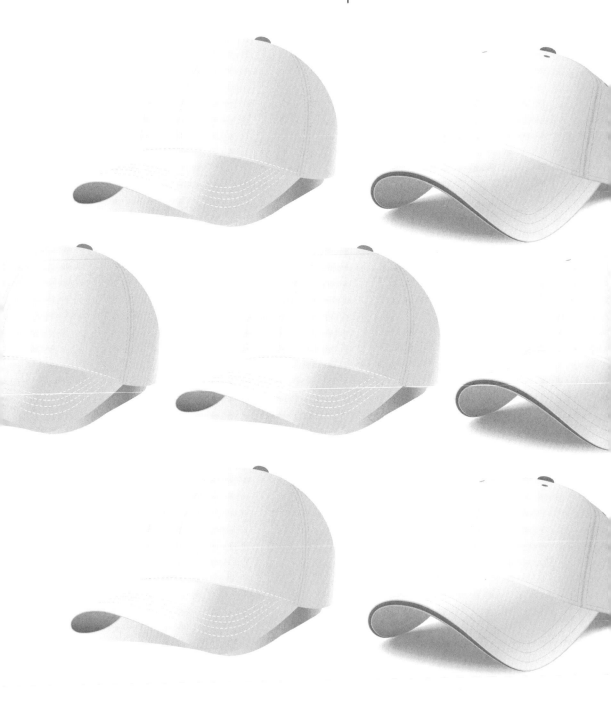

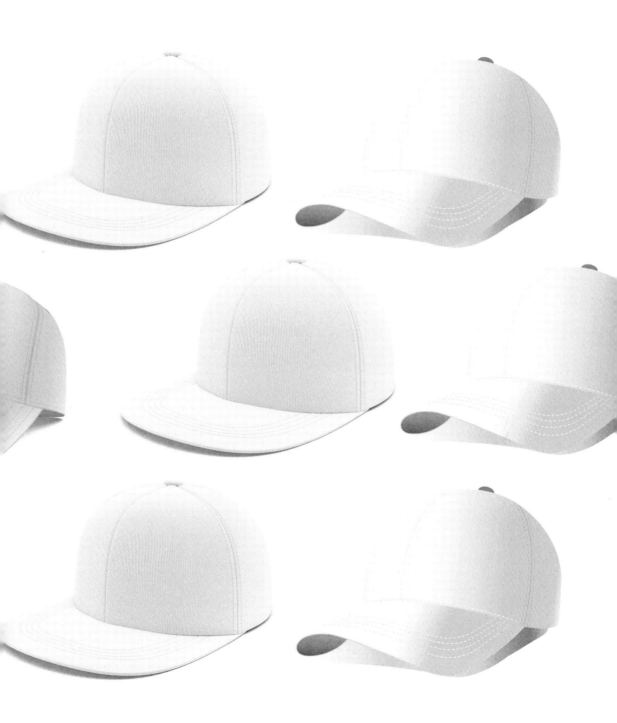

Put plenty of fish in the sea.

Extra! Extra! Today's front page needs a story.

Place an ad in the paper.

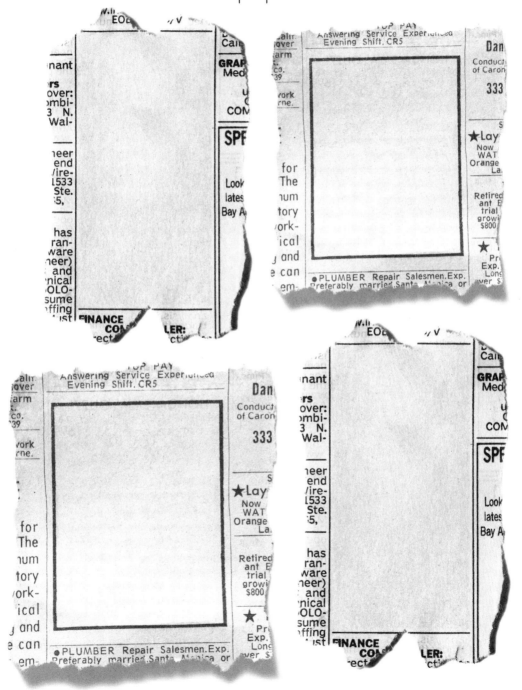

Somebody sent you some packages!
What's in them?

We've discovered some new types of moths and butterflies. What do they look like?

Coming soon to a theater near you . . .

What grows on these trees?

Create some spectacular sidewalk art.

Build your own bikes!

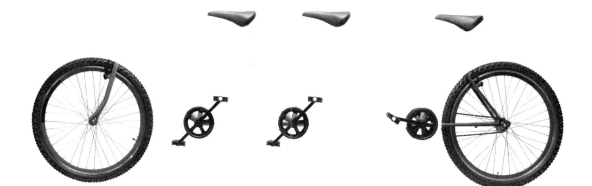

Who (or what!) is at the other end of the rope?

Finish the snowpeople before they melt!

What do you see in your crystal ball?

Who sent these postcards—and what do they say?

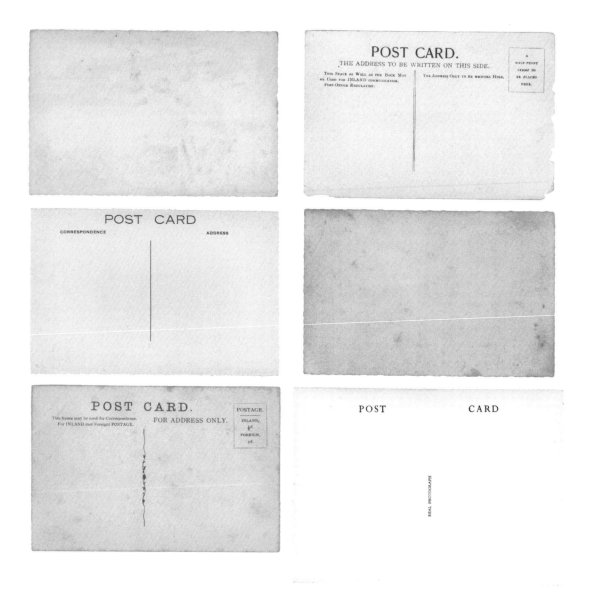

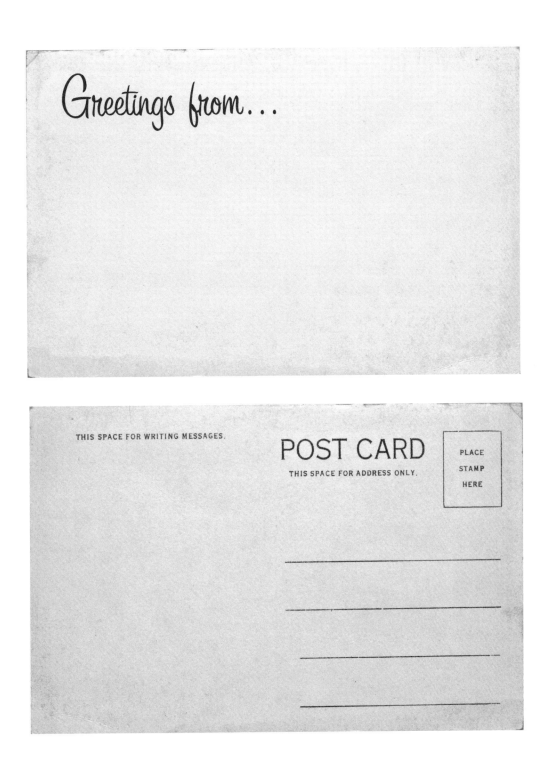

Greetings from...

POST CARD

THIS SPACE FOR ADDRESS ONLY.

PLACE
STAMP
HERE

Let's fly a kite!

What will be on
your business card?

Write a message in the sky.

What do you see out the airplane windows?

Draw the gnome a home.

These storybooks
need a story!

One large pizza with everything, please.
You add the toppings!

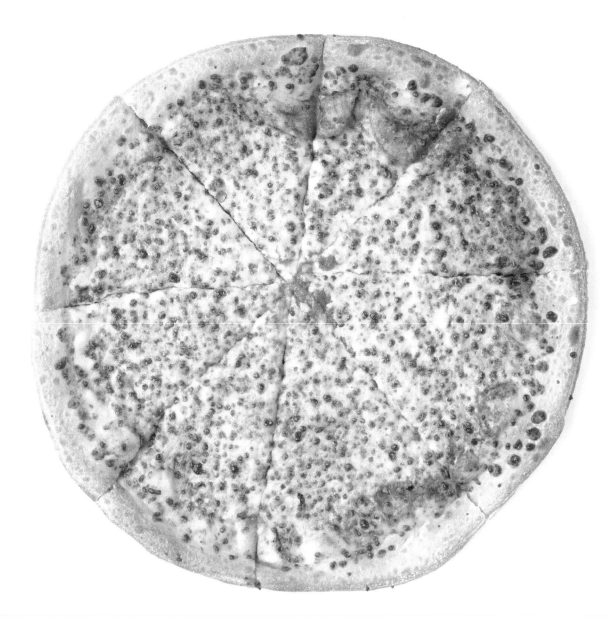

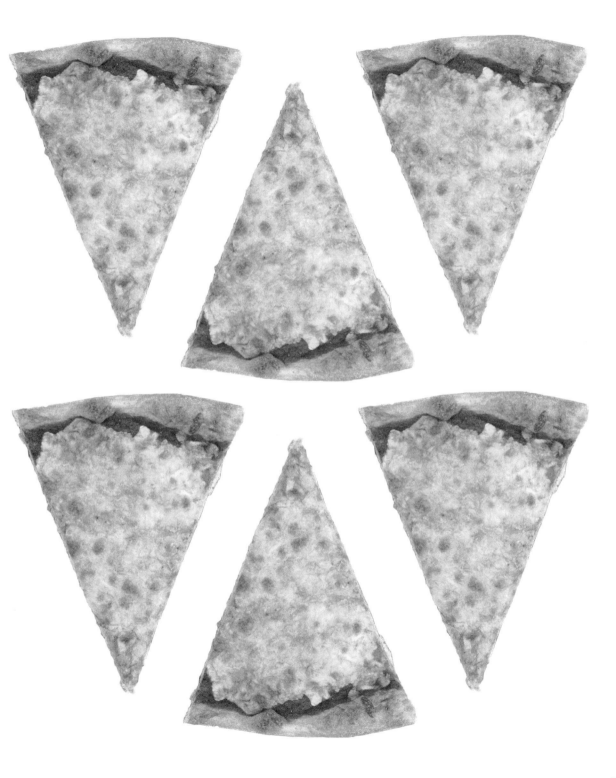

Welcome to the chemistry lab ...
What experiments will you do?

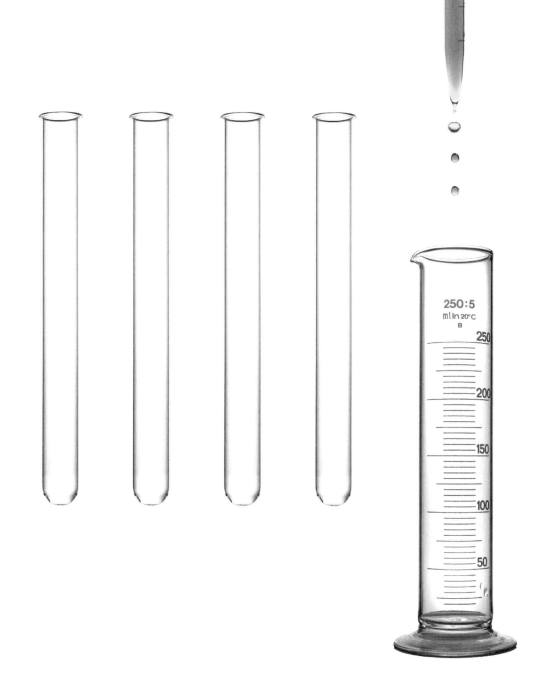

Your hamster looks bored ... Give him fun stuff
to do and friends to play with.

What can the circus seal balance on his nose?

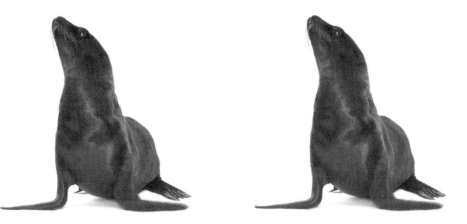

What's in your backyard?

Create the world's coolest T-shirts.

Post a note on the bulletin board.

Who's jumping on the bed?

Whose feet are these?

What are they juggling?

Who's climbing the mountain?

Draw the most delicious dinner ... or breakfast ...

or lunch . . . or dessert!

Build your dream house.

Thirsty? Invent some delicious drinks!

What do the posters say?

What outfit will the puppy wear today?

What do you see up high in the night sky?

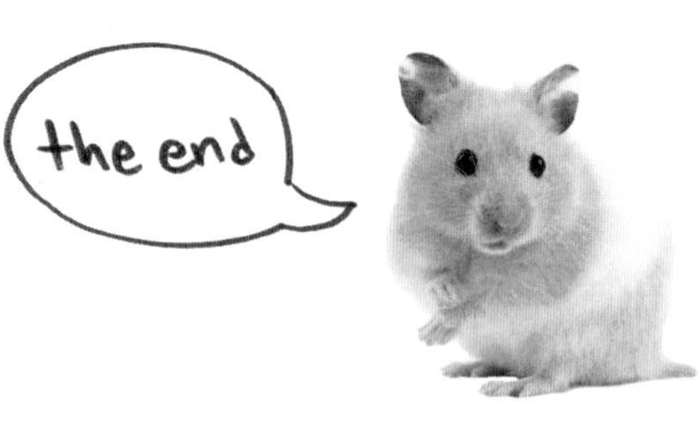
the end